Big Ange

Jamie Eastlake

I0141067

methuen | drama

LONDON • NEW YORK • OXFORD • NEW DELHI • SYDNEY

METHUEN DRAMA

Bloomsbury Publishing Plc, 50 Bedford Square, London, WC1B 3DP, UK
Bloomsbury Publishing Inc, 1359 Broadway, New York, NY 10018, USA
Bloomsbury Publishing Ireland, 29 Earlsfort Terrace, Dublin 2, D02 AY28, Ireland

BLOOMSBURY, METHUEN DRAMA and the Methuen
Drama logo are trademarks of Bloomsbury Publishing Plc

First published in Great Britain 2025

Copyright © Jamie Eastlake, 2025

Jamie Eastlake has asserted his right under the Copyright, Designs
and Patents Act, 1988, to be identified as Author of this work.

For legal purposes the Acknowledgements on p. xvii constitute an extension of this
copyright page.

Cover design by Holly Capper
Photography by Meg Jepson

A catalogue record for this book is available from the British Library.

A catalog record for this book is available from the Library of Congress.

ISBN: PB: 978-1-3506-1754-4
ePDF: 978-1-3506-1755-1
eBook: 978-1-3506-1985-2

Series: Modern Plays

Typeset by Westchester Publishing Services

To find out more about our authors and books visit
www.bloomsbury.com and sign up for our newsletters.

Big Ange

Jamie Eastlake

Cast and Creatives

Original version first performed at Live Theatre, Newcastle in November 2025.

Cast

STEVEN **Curtis Appleby**

Curtis Appleby is an award-winning actor from Gateshead, who studied at Italia Conti Academy of Arts (BA Hons Acting).

Credits include: *Roxy And Cy*, Vienna's English Theatre international tour; *Living on the Edge,* short film; *Offended,* film Sky Arts; *Hebburn,* BBC2.

'Curtis is super excited to be a part of *Big Ange*, and share this thought-provoking piece of theatre with audiences.'

CAROLINE **Erin Mullen**

Erin Mullen graduated from Guildhall School of Music and Drama in 2021. She was recently seen performing in *Gerry and Sewell* at the Newcastle Theatre Royal. She can now be seen in the feature film *The Last Breath*, playing the role of Riley. Before that Erin was seen in the ITV1 series *Midsomer Murders.*

ANGELA **Joann Condon**

Joann Condon's career began on the stage before moving into television and film. She has appeared in fantastic UK comedies and sitcoms, including *Little Britain* (BBC), where she was a regular as Fat Fighters attendee Pat. Other television credits include: *The Office* (BBC), *Dad's Army: The Lost Episodes* (BBC), *Edge of Heaven* (ITV), *Cradle to Grave* (BBC2) and *Harry Hill's Shark Infested Custard* (Avalon). Her screen work also includes roles in *Mrs Sidhu Investigates* (BBC) and the feature film *The Last Letter from Your Lover* (Netflix). Most recently, Joann wrote and starred in her acclaimed one-woman show *Little Boxes*, marking her debut as both writer and performer. The production was staged at Wimbledon Studios, Edinburgh Fringe and Adelaide Fringe.

DIRK **Gavin Webster**

Gavin Webster is a legendary, long-standing, influential yet unpredictable comedian from the North East of England. He's been going for over thirty years now. After making his modest debut in a pub in Gateshead in February 1993 he's done about 8,000 gigs from Aberdeen to Abu Dhabi, Manchester to Melbourne and Hartlepool to Hong Kong. Famed and respected by his peers for his uncompromising and unusual approach and distinctly original routines, he now boasts a large cult following around the country, at the Edinburgh Fringe and particularly on his native Tyneside where he sells out theatres with his one-man ninety-minute shows, not to mention fifteen full Edinburgh runs where he has a loyal following. Hard-edged routines, quick-fire pastiche pieces, moronic jokes and sardonic songs, his unique style has brought him this kind of praise and attention.

Gavin has also starred in a number of film and television programmes, including: *I, Daniel Blake* (Sixteen Films), *Sorry We Missed You* (Sixteen Films) and *Never Mind the Buzzcocks* (BBC2).

He has written for a number of comedians and TV personalities including Jason Manford. Gavin has also supported Sean Lock, Kevin Bridges, Jack Dee and Frankie Boyle on national tours.

@WEARETHEPEOPLEANDITSARMY **Lucy Eve Mann**

Lucy Eve Mann was born and bred in Middlesbrough and is very excited to perform once again in her own neck of the woods! She has recently finished a North West/East tour of Anna Jordan's play *Yen* in which she played the title character of Yen (also known as Jen). Lucy has appeared in several short films.

BOY **Ashen Hazel**

Ashen Hazel is an actor from Gateshead, who has been performing since he was a wee bairn over in Denmark. This is his professional debut.

Credits include: *Fresh Air,* National Theatre Connections with Theatre Royal Youth Company and *Chitty Chitty Bang Bang*, Starlight Theatre at Tyne Theatre and Opera House.

'Ashen is absolutely thrilled to join the *Big Ange* cast for this timely new production.'

Community Ensemble

Hope Ali, Rive Bertram, Dylan Duffy, Louie Graham, Evie Hogg, Adam Kareem, Poppy Keith, Robert Punchard and Lauren Sheperia.

With thanks to SA Performing Arts Centre, KEVI, Newcastle Sixth Form College and Gosforth Academy.

Creative Team

Director	**Jamie Eastlake**
Assistant Director	**Liv Byrom**
Movement Director	**Lucy Curry**
Set Design	**The Set Guise**
Sound Design	**Chris Prosho**
Lighting Design	**Drummond Orr**
Stage Manager	**Jade Young**
Technician	**Taylor Howie**
Technical Associate	**Ryan Olive**
Jackie Producer	**Rosie Bowden**
Assistant Producer	**Pavla Rumenova**
Photography	**Meg Jepson**
Key Art Designer	**Jenny Nicholas**
Dramaturgical Support	**Laura Lindow, John Hickman**

For Live Theatre

Executive Director/ Joint Chief Executive	**Jacqui Kell**
Artistic Director/ Joint Chief Executive	**Jack McNamara**
PA to Joint Chief Executives	**Alex Redman**

Creative Programme

New Work Producer	**JD Stewart**
Artist Development Producer	**John Dawson**
Associate Artist	**gobscure**
Associate Artist	**Kemi-Bo Jacobs**

Children and Young People

CYPP Leader   **Helen Green**
Senior Creative   **Paul James**
   Associate CYPP
Creative Lead Live Tales   **Becky Morris**

Technical Production

Production Manager   **Drummond Orr**
Technical and Digital Manager   **Chris Prosho**
Technician   **Taylor Howie**
Estates and Maintenance Assistant   **Ken Evans**

Operations and Finance

Finance and Operations Manager   **Antony Robertson**
Finance and Payroll Officer   **Catherine Moody**
Fundraising and   **Alison Nicholson**
   Development Manager

Marketing and Communications

Marketing and   **Lisa Campbell and**
   Communications Managers   **Michele McCallion**
Marketing and   **Arthur Roberts**
   Communications Officer

Customer Services and Box Office

House and Estates Manager   **Kirsten Dixon**
Deputy House and   **Michael Davies and**
   Estates Managers   **Patrycja Nowacka**
Duty Manager and   **Alicia Meehan,**
   Bar Supervisors   **Jake Wilson Craw,**
                                  Caitlin Fairlamb and
                                  Tyler Gatenby
Customer Services Assistant   **Lukas Gabryseh,**
   and Bar Supervisors   **Hannah Guthrie,**
                                  Owen Saunders,

	Hendrika Seguro-Bigg and Ruth Sheldon
Customer Services Assistants	Amy Becke, Hope Brown-King, Elisha Ewing, Amy Foster, Elspeth Frith, Jay Hildreth, Nathan Jones, Reece Lumsden, Lucy Marsh, Bridget Marumo, Sidney Moshe Phoebus, Isabella Seale, Amber Smith, Chan Ward-Mercer and Kathryn Watt
Box Office Assistants	Daniel Ball, Asa Beckett, Steven Blackshaw, Joseph Duffy, Sarah Matthews, Ruby Taylor and Jasper Wilding
Housekeeping	**Wendy Denny, Lydia Igbinosa and Camille Vitorino-Itoua Angela Salem**

For Newcastle Theatre Royal

Chief Executive	**Marianne Locatori**
Director of Audience and Communications	**Jo Kirby**

Director of Creative Development	**Kim Hoffmann**
Director of Finance	**Colin Johnston**
Director of Operations	**Siobhan Lightfoot**
Head of Business Support	**Alex Grieves**
Head of Development	**Kelly Smith**
Head of Experience	**Aynsley Cowan-Young**
Head of Marketing	**Gillian Northey**
Head of People	**Aurora Kerr**
Head of Technical and Maintenance	**Nathan Reynard**
Head of Ticketing and Revenue	**Annabel Robson**

JAMIE EASTLAKE

Jamie is a working class Olivier award-winning theatre-maker from Blyth, Northumberland. A constant advocate for working class representation in theatre who has been involved in this conversation nationally across various forms of media and parliament. Jamie has been mentored by Royal Court Theatre artistic director David Byrne, and is currently producer at Eastlake Productions, who work in partnership with Newcastle Theatre Royal. As a playwright his writing credits include: *Gerry and Sewell* (Live Theatre/Newcastle Theatre Royal); *Artful Dodgers* (National Theatre Studio, co-writer with John Hickman); *Monkey's Blood* (Vault Festival); *Harold and Keith attempt to use zoom to discuss the potential takeover of beloved football club Newcastle United – An Opera* (OperaVision). As a theatre-producer he produced *Flesh and Bone* (Soho Theatre) which won the Olivier award for outstanding achievement in an affiliate theatre with Unpolished Theatre; *This Not Culturally Significant* (Vault Festival/Gilded Balloon); *FCUK'D* (Bunker Theatre) as well as over fifty other productions across the UK and Europe. Selected directing credits include: *Gerry and Sewell* (Newcastle Theatre Royal); *Ghosts of Metroland* (Live Theatre); *Artful Dodgers* (National Theatre Studio) and *Your Ever Loving* (Underbelly). He became the youngest person running a theatre venue in the country in 2015 when he set up Theatre N16 in London. The theatre went on to programme over 300 pieces of work and became a groundbreaking stomping ground for a host of new work. He was Associate Producer at Live Theatre from 2019 to 2020, co-founder of Laurel's Theatre in North Tyneside, and has been nominated for over a dozen OffWestEnd Awards. Jamie bleeds Black and White.

@jamieeastlake

https://www.jamieeastlake.com

Eastlake Productions

Eastlake Productions are North East theatre-makers based in Newcastle upon Tyne. We strive to make bold and important work for the region.

We have produced over fifty different productions across Europe, most recently the upscaling of *Gerry and Sewell* from Laurel's, Whitley Bay to Newcastle Theatre Royal.

Eastlake Productions are currently working in partnership with Newcastle Theatre Royal. We are consultant producers on the Open Door programme, which strives to support new and developing professional work and provide professional development opportunities for actors, writers, artists, designers and makers from the region.

@eastlakeproductions

https://www.eastlakeproductions.co.uk

Live Theatre

'One of the most fertile crucibles of new writing' *The Guardian*

Our vision is for a North East that writes its own story and fights for a more creative future.

Live Theatre occupies a unique place as one of the country's only dedicated new writing buildings outside of London. Across its fifty-one-year history it has launched the careers of many of today's leading theatre figures and continues to develop and platform the artists of tomorrow, from playwrights to local school children. Deeply connected to its region and unafraid to confront the most pressing issues of our time, Live Theatre brings ambitious regional artists and adventurous local audiences into vivid contact.

Our mission is to unearth the rich and unexpected narratives of our region, to nurture creativity and bring passionate ideas to life and to be a space that unites people and ignites imaginations.

'Live Theatre has supported generation after generation of new writers, actors and theatre artists.' **Lee Hall, Playwright**

@livetheatrenewcastle

https://www.live.org.uk

Theatre Royal

Newcastle upon Tyne

Newcastle Theatre Royal

Newcastle Theatre Royal is an independent large-scale Theatre. As a charitable trust it runs one of only nine Grade 1 Listed theatres in England. There are two performance spaces. In the 1,247 seat Theatre Royal auditorium it presents a broad and ambitious programme, encompassing the finest of West End, national and international drama, musicals, pantomime, comedy, opera and dance for audiences across the North East and beyond.

The Studio, a newly refurbished seventy-four seat space, is dedicated to supporting, developing and nurturing emerging artists and theatre-makers to create new work that reflects the rich cultural heritage and vibrant spirit of Newcastle alongside being a space for the Creative Engagement programme.

Regularly partnering with West End producer Michael Harrison, Newcastle Theatre Royal has recently opened *Bedknobs and Broomsticks* prior to a UK tour, *The Drifters Girl* prior to the West End, launched a new pantomime *Pinocchio* and will premiere a second new pantomime titled *The Little Mermaid* later this year.

Expanding creative partnerships in 2024 Newcastle Theatre Royal co-produced two productions; the critically acclaimed *Pride and Prejudice* (*sort of)* with David Pugh prior to a national tour and *Gerry and Sewell* with Eastlake Productions, a new play based on the cult Geordie film *Purely Belter*.

Beyond the stage, Newcastle Theatre Royal plays a vital role in the community, offering an extensive Creative Engagement programme that inspires, educates and engages with young people, communities and schools from across the region. The largest programme of its kind in the North East, this work sits at the heart of the theatre's creative ambition providing participants with pathways to find their own creativity, supporting both personal and professional development.

Talent development and community participation partnerships with national visiting companies such as the Royal Shakespeare Company, New Adventures and the National Theatre, ensure this outreach and engagement work is embedded in the creative programme on stage.

Creative Engagement programme highlights include Project A, a fulltime, year-long, dedicated actor training programme for 18–25 year olds, with over 90% of the 130 young people who have graduated going onto work professionally, secure professional representation or successfully audition for Drama school. A partnership with WEST (West End Schools Trust) supports a regular programme of workshops for children in Years 3–6 to develop oracy, literacy and communication skills and provides opportunities to see a range of performances at the Theatre. The Theatre Royal Youth Programme (TRY) engages annually with 1,500 young people aged 5–19 through regular after-school classes, workshops and summer schools.

@newcastletheatreroyal

https://www.theatreroyal.co.uk

A Note From The Writer

What is right? What will be left?

The world feels like a scary place right now.
But maybe it always has been.

Only now, the horrors – both distant and local – are in our pockets. At our
fingertips. Every single day.
That constant connection breeds division. Hyperbole.
Fear that feels bigger than it's ever been.

I'm scared.
Scared for my little girl growing up in this world.
And that's before I even begin to consider the colour of her skin.

Do I have answers?
Not a fucking clue.

When Live Theatre asked me, 'What are you working on?'
I looked at the slate of projects I've got on: big, bold, crowd-pleasing
stories aimed at massive stages.

Then I glanced at the back of my notebook.
Scribbles. An idea. A dinner lady.
Maybe she ends up coaching the school football team? A daft
notion, really.
Something about how the Tottenham manager's nickname sounds more
like something a dinner lady would call herself while serving fish fingers.

But it kept tugging at me.

Alongside that were more scattered thoughts:
How do I define myself politically right now?
A child of Blairism.
A grandson of Unionism.
A boy from Blyth (not that one).
A constant pain in my mates' arses when I bring up politics during pint
number six in the Malaga sun.

This play was born out of bafflement.
It's meant to feel like that.
It's about being scared and confused –
But wrapped in the warm, fierce hug of a working-class woman who's
just trying to do her bit.

Fighting her own battle.
A battle to save young men.

And why is it down to a woman to do that?
I don't know.
It just is, isn't it?

Because when you look around – it is young men.
Young men shouting the loudest on podcasts.
Young men with boots on the ground and flags you have to double-check in the history books.
Young men shooting at presidents and influencers.
Young men who become old men who stir up hysteria, press the war buttons, push the narratives of hate.

And then, on the other side, there's the self-righteous left:
'If you're not sharing this, you're not an ally.'
Thanks for the TED Talk.
Did you check if the glue you used to stick yourself to the M25 was made from horse bones after you posted about cancelling the Grand National?

Have we ever been this divided?

This play doesn't have answers.
But it wants to ask questions.
To start a conversation.
To make you look across the room and say, 'Why?'

If you've picked this up and given it a read – thank you.
If you're watching it in a theatre – thank you.
I hope it makes you feel something.

It's meant to be a bit mental.
Because life is a bit mental right now.
But maybe – just maybe – it can help us talk to each other again.

I couldn't keep dragging my pals into this heavy mess every time we go for a pint.

So here's a play instead

Up the Mags. Solidarity forever.

Jamie Eastlake

Acknowledgments

Always make sure your heroes are super. These are mine. And I can't thank them enough for various lush reasons. There's ten (so plus me in goal it makes a cracking starting eleven).

Jade and Zia ❤

My Mam

Darren Eales

George Caulkin

David Byrne

Rosie Bowden

Marianne Locatori

John Hickman

Big Dan Burn

And my lush friends and family (they know who they are) who made sure I saw through the night.

Big Ange

Jamie Eastlake

Cast of Characters

Angela, a dinner lady, 50s, from North London. Snuggly.
Steven, 18, from Blyth. On the edge.
Caroline, 23, from Blyth, since moved to London. On the edge.
@WeAreThePeopleAndItsArmy, a masked figure from the internet. Over the edge.
Ange Postecoglou, Tottenham Hotspur Manager, Australian. Lush.
Dirk the DJ, older. Wheeler-dealer.
The Boy, 16. Sick of listening to Ange's stories. Hopeful.
The Girl, a radical left rioter. Opening.

An ensemble of school kids/The dancing boys/
The Newsham Lads/Dinosaurs/The London Geezers,
Journalist, TV Reporter played by an ensemble
and potentially played by the actor playing
@WeAreThePeopleAndItsArmy.

Production Notes

The stage can be vast and bare. The world is opaque and punctuated with the moments of the story. Therefore, the stage in a smaller space without wing space can be cluttered with the different settings as long as there is space for the movement of the dancing boys. The furniture in the world is opaque and therefore can be just played with potential mounds of astro turf, not sofas and chairs etc.

Act One

Scene 1

A song plays. Loreen, 'Euphoria'. It's dramatic.

The Girl *enters.*

She sings the opening lines from Avicci's 'Hey Brother'.

She gestures to herself.

Continues, singing the end of the first verse of 'Hey Brother'.

She throws a brick through a window and writes in red spray paint on the wall. 'Liars.'

Strings. Then an alarm. Daunting. **The Girl** *exits.*

On the stage . . .

A massive wind turbine. Looking down like a god.

A piece of art. 'The Spirit of the Staithes.'

This place that once had purpose. A boarded-up shop.

A mural of a footballer on a fish and chip shop wall.

This place is Blyth.

A few bits of graffiti adorn the walls.

'Local homes for local people.'

And a Paddington Bear 'Migration is not a crime.'

The stage is a football pitch but the lines are red and make a cross like a sort of fucked up St George's flag.

A boy enters. In a football kit. A tripod under his arm. 18. **Steven**.

Around him an array of other footballers surround him. Dancing boys.

He hits the spotlight. Euphoria.

The footballers dance around him. He is stoic. Loving it.

They dance.

A girl enters. 23. She carries a baby. **Caroline**.

The footballers gather around her. In a mating call.

She hits the spotlight. Holds up the baby like Simba. Euphoria.

They dance.

The lights centre.

A figure appears. Smoke. Lasers.

The works.

A dinner lady. Angela. **50s**. *She spins the decks. Controlling the movements of everyone.*

It's madness.

Steven *takes control of the boys, they snarl as he lights a Molotov cocktail.*

Angela *exits from the DJ booth. A swift noise.*

Caroline   Stop.

Steven   I can't.

Caroline   Think of everything we talked about.

Steven   I'm doing it for her.

Caroline   Please.

Steven   You don't understand.

Caroline   They're all lying. To you. Like I said.

Steven   You're still lecturing me. You're still doing it. Send me on my way!

Caroline   I . . . this is not how this is meant to end . . .

Scene 2

A flat in Blyth.

A few months earlier.

Steven *is sitting watching a film. He's cuddling a large dinosaur soft toy/cushion thing.*

Caroline *enters with a pushchair.*

Steven *continues watching the film.*

Caroline   Evening.

Steven   What you doing back?

Steven *hides the dinosaur soft toy/cushion thing behind the sofa.*

Caroline   Not allowed to visit, like?

Steven   Aye but . . .

Steven *realises his niece is in the pram.*

He grabs her out.

Steven   You are though! How's Uncle Steven's little angel?!

He puts her down and blows a raspberry on her tummy.

Caroline   Were you just cuddling Rexy?

Steven   Don't know what you're talking about.

Caroline *goes behind the sofa and pulls out the dinosaur soft toy/ cushion thing.*

She gives **Steven** *a mischievous eye.*

Steven   It's for me neck. Support.

Steven *throws it once more behind the sofa.*

Caroline   Where's Dad?

Steven   Masons.

Caroline   Who with?

Steven   I daint kna, Rossy or a bird. (*Beat.*) Probably a bird.

Caroline   A woman, Steven. Not a bird. A woman.

Steven   Areet calm ya passions. I wouldn't ever describe the lasses Dad goes out with as 'Women'.

Caroline   You're something, you know that.

Steven   I'm just saying they're not classy. Get off your high horse, man.

Caroline   What, he's seeing more than one?

Steven   Look, he's just playing the field. Keeping his options open.

Caroline   The field? It's not a pack of antelopes he's hunting.

Steven   Get a grip of yourself, man. I didn't mean owt by it.

A silence.

Caroline   How's school?

Steven   Fine.

Caroline   The footy?

Steven   Shite. We've won one of the last ten. Newsham have beaten us twice this season. No Wensleydale side has ever lost twice in a season to Newsham. We'll not be able to set foot in Blyth town centre if we don't smash them in the inter-town summer cup.

Caroline   Aye, but it's not as if you and your pals have a Dan Burn amongst you.

Steven   Ah, so you are still at least watching the Toon? And actually, I'd say there's three or four of the lads who have a chance. Dang's a hell of a winger and Jagdish is still scoring like nowt's the matter.

Caroline   Well, I've seen the Champions League games, watched them in this lush pub on the Thames called the Ship, in Wandsworth Town.

Steven   With the new lad?

Caroline   He's not a lad, he's thirty-six. And no, he watches the rugby, I've just caught a glimpse of the matches when we've been in there, that's all. Besides, I don't have time with this one, the new job and the amount of marches we've been on.

Steven   Ah whey, it's good. Good to have some happiness back.

A moment.

Caroline   You should see the amount of people who were out with us this weekend on Whitehall, it was so inspiring. Felt like we were properly doing something.

Steven *ignores her and continues watching the telly.*

Caroline   And next week we're doing a fundraiser . . .

Steven'*s phone rings. He answers it.*

Steven   Aye, yeah, nah, sweet, aye, aye. Tada tada.

He puts the phone away.

Caroline   Rude.

Steven   Was just Dad. Saying he was probably gonna stop out, there's some eggs in the fridge. Luckily I have his card details on me JustEat.

Caroline   Has he said who he's voting for?

Nothing from **Steven**.

Caroline   Just, I know this has always been a Labour family because of Grandad but I hope he's seriously thinking about altern . . .

Steven (*inter.*)   Caroline, man. Can you just drop it for one second. We know you like politics and saving the planet. And helping all the poor foreign bairns and that's very kind and lovely. But can the freak who used to give is a dutch oven just have a normal conversation with is?

Caroline   What the fuck is a dutch oven?

Steven   You know, when you used to fart in me duvet and lock me up in it. Matilda or Ice age?

Caroline   I'm not about silly games anymore. I'm sorry my mind's been opened a bit from leaving here.

Beat

And I never did that. That's some dreamworld you're thinking of.

Steven   I'm eighteen. I want to finish watching this Bond film. I haven't spoken to Dad about politics this week. My main focus right now is figuring out why I thought media was a good subject to focus on and how anyone from the arse-end of Northumberland can make films for a living.

Caroline   What about the A-star you got in your poetry module?

Steven   Wey aye, that's gonna help me get a job in Blyth, isn't it?

Beat.

And what would you like from Julietta's – kebab and bolognese pizza with garlic sauce like always?

Caroline   Steven. I'm a fucking vegan. Listen.

Steven   I'll order you some lettuce then.

Caroline *grabs her child and goes to leave.*

Steven   And don't go in a huff upstairs. Dad is just having a bit of fun. We don't have to start the next revolution right this instant.

She leaves.

Steven   And don't be leaving me a dutch oven!

He chuckles to himself.

Scene 3

'Kentucky Woman' by Neil Diamond plays.

Angela *enters.*

She's dressed as Colonel Sanders the KFC man.

Some kids enter.

She hands out school dinner trays with buckets of chicken on them.

She's loving it.

The kids are confused. The song stops.

The Boy   Ange, man. Can you just be normal for once.

Angela   You'll look back at these days and they'll be the best days of your life.

The Boy *tries to leave.*

Angela *puts her arm around him keeping in his spot.*

He sighs, knowingly. She does shit like this a lot.

Angela (*cont.*)   I thought I'd dress like the KFC man and serve the chicken from buckets today. You know, to make you all smile. You see, I've noticed a massive amount of kids not being kids these last few years. Especially the lads. A lot more anger and sadness. I have a theory that it started in 2005.

She strokes her Colonel Sanders beard knowingly.

Go and ask Moira in the back for Ange's whiteboard, would you. That's a good lad.

The Boy *exits.*

The Boy *enters with a whiteboard, covering the whole of it is a picture of Jamie Oliver that's been defaced.*

Angela   Thank you, young man.

Angela   A long long time ago. I can still remember. How that food used to make them smile. And I knew if I had my chance. That I could make them all dance. Maybe they'd be happy for a while. But Oliver made me shiver. With every plate I'd deliver. Bad news on the doorstep. I couldn't take one more step. I do remember that I cried. When he chastised how much we fried. But something touched them deep inside. The day. Turkey twizzlers. Died.

The Boy   I swear that was another song.

Angela   Never mind that. You can go and have your lunch now.

The Boy *exits*.

Angela   And then Blair goes, gorgeous Gordon follows, and in come the Tories with their austerity. No wonder the bairns looked so miserable – their parents strung up to dry while the country was told to 'tighten its belt'.

Bairns. Am I saying that right? Twenty years up here and I still don't trust myself with it. Where I grew up – Tottenham Hale – we just said sprogs. Rugrats. Nothing to do with the cartoon. Though, mind, American culture was all over our house. Neil Diamond blasting from me dad's LPs. He always said, 'Real music's sung by men in blue jeans and sunglasses.' So aye, I still wear denim on Thursdays for him. We had two dogs, boxers they were – Calvin and Klein.

Beat

Us. The bairns. The working classes. Always pitted against each other. Austerity. Then Brexit. Then Covid. Then more austerity. And Boris. Nee wonder the lads are angry. We Londoners knew he was a divvy twenty years back.

But it's not just the lads, is it? The lasses see the brunt of it. That's why I do this. This get-up. This daft energy. My theory is if I can bring a bit of light into their lives, maybe, just maybe, I can change one of their paths. You never know, do you?

Next week I'm planning a DJ night. Got inspired watching a documentary about a troubled young lad, Tim – massive DJ, ended tragically. And I know the boys love DJs. So if one of them feels a spark, a chance at something bigger, then maybe they won't get lost in the anger.

So aye – it might just be one night of lights and decks and daftness. But if it saves even one of them, then it's worth every ounce of me. And it's a big distraction from those elections coming. I hope Labour get back in. That Starmer's dad was a tool-maker, you know.

The Boy *enters and puts his tray on a pile.*

The Boy   Avicci, Tim's DJ name, it was Avicci.

Angela   Excellent timing. You can wheel that back to Moira for me.

The Boy *wheels the whiteboard off showing the back of it with a huge photo of Gordon Brown in a heart and sparkles. Very odd.*

Angela   Right. Suppose I better start to learn to spin some decks.

Avicci 'Wake Me Up' plays.

Angela *wheels out a trolly full of bargain buckets.*

Scene 4

Blyth town centre.

Steven *enters, kicking a ball, a tripod on his shoulder.*

He sets it up with his iPhone as the camera and sits on the ball.

Steven   If it's good enough for Danny Boyle to shoot a whole film on it's good enough for Steven Mooney and his two-k TikTok followers.

He sets up a microphone on his collar.

Steven   Testing, testing.

He looks around to see if nobody is there.

One two, check the mic, yessai.

He awkwardly readjusts himself.

No young Geordie lad can speak into a mic and not do that.

He starts to film, panning the tripod.

A Turkish barbers. A nail salon. Cash Converters. Ladbrokes. Another Turkish barbers. (*Beat.*) It's not exactly viral content, is it.

He stops filming and sees something.

A family walk down the high street. The mam wears a face covering, the youngest boy is creasing, he's so happy. I go to film. In the Cash Converters' window, a figure of Daniel Craig as Bond points his gun in my direction. I think of my favourite 007 moments. Skyfall on ITV2 last night. I planned the shot. Past the stores and boarded up ones and ending with the family. They're so happy amidst it all. I shoot.

He places a small speaker down and presses play. 'Tennyson' by Thomas Newman plays. He pans the camera and speaks into the mic.

We are not now that strength which in old days moved earth and heaven, that which we are we are one equal temper of heroic hearts, made weak by time and fate, but strong in will, to strive to seek to find and not to yield.

A moment. He watches his video back.

That was bloody class. Hashtag This is Britain. Hashtag Blyth. Hashtag Bond. I'll post it on my TikTok.

Scene 5

'Jerusalema' by Master KG and Nomcebo Zikode plays.

Angela *enters, she's followed by several backing dancers. Different people from Blyth. A butcher, a few old dears, a Blyth Spartans fan etc.*

They dance. Obviously.

Angela   During the 'P' word [pandemic] I joined in every single group activity I could. My hands were bloody red raw from all the doorstep clapping.

Dirk, *in his 60s a bit bedraggled, enters from the crowd.*

Dirk   Nobody slaps their palms together like Ange does!

Dirk *spits on the floor and exits into the crowd.*

Angela   That was my neighbour, Dirk, two doors down. Cracking lad. Has a mobile disco company and a few other businesses. Bit of a Del Boy. Knew me dad.

Dirk *re-enters from the crowd.*

Dirk   If ya need owt doing, I'm ya man. 'You need something to work, pick up the blower and buzz Dirk.' Much better than 'Autoglass repair, Autoglass replace', isn't it?

Dirk *disappears back into the dancers.*

Angela   In those dark days I managed to convince over half of Albatross Way to learn this dance. Nowt beats a bit of community dancing to scare away a deadly virus!

My dad used to say – 'You've got dark thoughts? Have a dance with your peers. You're angry at the world? You and your best pals put on some tap shoes.

Scared? Get round the old people's home and get them thrusting.'

The song switches to something sexy. The dancers become elderly people.

They dance. Sexily.

The song ends abruptly.

The dancers leave.

Angela   Maybe don't do the last one. Nye Bevan House management no longer send me a Christmas card after I had Eileen and Margaret doing a routine to Tatu 'All the Things She Said'.

A beat.

Anyway I'd pulled in some favours for the DJ night. Dirk brought all his disco equipment down.

Dirk the DJ *re-enters.*

Dirk   I've packed the full works. An Allen and Heath SQ5, a Sennheiser ew 5000 G4, a Behringer SD16, a full fogging machine for atmosphere, and I've set three pyros for the last number. Big glittery bastards they are.

He spits on the floor and exits.

Angela   Christine from the food bank had some cracking black drapes to cover the hall. Jackie from Rumps bar volunteered to make non-alcoholic cocktails and set up a little bar area. And the trolley lads from Asda created a shuttle service from the car park to the hall, you know to add a little fun to the proceedings. The kids would be dropped off at the gates and there'd be a trolley waiting for them with a chauffer suit-cladded trolley lad ready to push them in it, with a high viz on of course! Dirk had set me up this cracking booth to spin the decks from.

Dirk *re-enters.*

Dirk   I normally save these for people's weddings, but I'm always there for Ange after all she's done for me. 'If planning your big day seems like an irk, pick up the blower and buzz Dirk.'

He spits on the floor and exits.

Angela   I'd spent every night for two weeks making a papier-mache piñata pig that I filled with sweets. Jamie Oliver would have been furious. Bastard. And to make the boys have a giggle I put a Newsham footy top on the pig. Newsham is our school, Wensleydale's enemy. I was perched on top of the school's theatre stage. I'd even fashioned myself a pair of glitter joggers. Bought the sequins in bulk from a bankrupt magician's warehouse.

Angela *gets into her DJ booth.*

Angela   This was it. These boys needed joy, and I was going to serve it by the ladle. Boys! Girls! Gays! Um . . . Lays.

Angela *slips up, she means well.*

Dirk *re-enters, whispers in* **Angela**'s *ear.*

Dirk   Theys.

Angela   That's it, sorry, bit nervous everyone.

Beat.

Everything started without a hitch. I started, obviously, with some Avicci but then mixed into some more modern classics.

Gina G 'Just a Little Bit' plays.

Angela   My theory being that if you give a taste of the 90s then the youngins would be transported back to happier times. You know Brit Pop, Rule Britannia, proper school dinners! Jackie was spinning the cocktail shakers like there was no tomorrow, some of the older kids started dancing in pairs. A couple of the upper sixth form, two lads, they danced really close, staring into each other's eyes. It was so bloody cute. I even saw some of the footy lads around them giving them the thumbs up and applauding. Kids can be cruel but in the right environment, kids can also be very kind. My sequins glistened in the lights, bouncing glimmer across the floor, like a tidal wave of nostalgic glam, sparkling hope into the hearts of forgotten young men. No matter who you were, you were free, enjoy yourself, feel part of something, be happy and let yourself go, darling.

Angela *leads a dance. Again. She sings the chorus.*

Angela   Then a rumble. From outside of the hall. Coming closer. And closer. My pint of council pop on my booth started to shake, like a T-Rex was approaching. Closer and closer. Until . . . The doors broke open and several of the chauffer shopping trolleys came flying through the door.

Several shopping trolleys pushed with a few radgie boys in them enter.

The Boy   It's the fucking Newsham footy team!

Angela   Then it was complete bedlam.

Gina G continues to play.

Angela   Trolleys were used as battering rams. Jackie from Rumps bar taken clear out mid way through a mocktail mojito.

Dirk *enters.*

Dirk   Ange! Set off the big bastard pyros! Scare off the little shits!

Angela   I was frozen in panic. I watched as Dirk was close lined by two of the Newsham lads, falling deep into the crowd of boys as arms and legs became one, punches flying left, right and centre, Jackie from Rumps bar screaming 'My eyes, there's lime juice in me eyes!' 'Ange! Shut it down!' I pressed the pyros button, or what I thought was the pyros button, but nothing happened . . . for a second. But then the papier-mache pig I had spent the last two weeks making full of sweets came swinging down, swinging down in its Newsham footy top, a stupid attempt I'd made to create a bit of camaraderie with all the sporty lads.

A Newsham Lad   She's fucking taking the piss, isn't she?

Angela   That didn't go down well with our guests. They ripped it up, completely decimated it, I swear one of them just using his teeth, it was like scene from Lord of the Flies and my Piggy was dying just as savagely. Dirk sprung out of the mould of madness, a flair in one hand, smoke filtering up and up and up, roaring red, I couldn't help but think of Chris Pratt in Jurassic World with the velociraptors, or Indy entering the tomb before the boulder incident, but this was Dirk. Fifty-seven-years-old, covered in sweat and pink bits of papier-mache.

Dirk   Shut it down, Ange! The plugs!

Angela   I knew it was game over. I knew I had failed. I saw the spider's web of cables in the wall off the stage and I pulled them out, Gina G coming to an abrupt popping halt. I thought I'd saved them. With sequins. With a pig. With Gina G. But sometimes daft isn't enough. Sometimes daft breaks.

Scene 6

A flat in Blyth.

Caroline *sits. Her baby asleep beside her.*

Steven *enters.*

Caroline   I'm thinking we could all go on a walk later on, to Plessey Woods. Go to the stepping stones.

Steven *is engrossed in his phone.*

Steven   Aye aye aye.

Caroline   The commons at Clapham are lovely. But there's nothing beats a proper wood in Northumberland. Do you remember when we were younger, you were probably only like four or five and Mam would bring us with a massive picnic. Dairylea Lunchables, we'd see who could build the biggest ones like Scooby and Shaggy. Babybels, Viennese whirls.

Steven   Aye and you would mush up the Viennese whirl in your mouth and chase me round the trees trying to spit it on me. Dirty bitch.

Caroline   Never happened.

Steven *is still engrossed in his phone.*

Caroline   Who you sexting?

Steven   Video I made last week has went mental.

He shows **Caroline** *his phone.*

Caroline   Wahey. My brother's famous.

She looks at it again and snatches it out his hand.

Steven   What you doing?

Caroline *is aghast at what she sees on the phone screen.*

Caroline   Steven, the fucking accounts. The people commenting. Full on fucking vermin.

Steven   Areet, calm down, man, how are they that bad?

Caroline   Union Jack flags and AI photos of lions and Stephen Yaxley-Lennon with massive muscles, man. Fucking hell. What have you said in this video?

Steven   It's literally a shot of the town centre with some poetry over it and a young lad laughing at the end of it. I thought people were just liking it as it felt real.

Caroline   Let's see it.

The video plays out.

Steven (*on the video*)   We are not now that strength which in old days moved earth and heaven, that which we are we are one equal temper of heroic hearts, made weak by time and fate, but strong in will, to strive to seek to find and not to yield.

A moment of silence.

Caroline *is thinking.*

Caroline   Fuck's sake. Can you not see what you've done, you fucking idiot.

Steven   I shot a real life video of what the town centre looks like and then filmed a family with a boy creasing.

Caroline   And who are that family?

Steven   I dunno . . .

Caroline   The mam's wearing a niqab. So a Muslim family. Come on, put two and two together.

Steven   What are you talking about? I filmed exactly what I saw!

Caroline   Broken Britain. A high street in decline. Boarded up shops. And then a happy Muslim following it. You're the one who wants to be a filmmaker, what's that story say?

Steven   It's just something poetic. It's the poem from Bond, from Skyfall that M says. Tennyson. I . . .

Caroline   Fuck sake, you fucking idiot.

Steven   Stop calling me a fucking idiot! Just because you think you're better than I am doesn't make me a fucking idiot! Stop telling me I'm making stories up from when we were younger, stop making me feel tiny, stop, stop, stop and just listen for once man. Matilda or Ice Age???

Caroline   Fuck you, we're not kids anymore, playing stupid games like that. You're messed up. I'm going for a walk.

Steven   It hasn't changed, you know. I still wonder what comes next. What chance I actually have. Bright lad. Zero fucking prospects!

Caroline *exits with the baby.*

Steven *looks at his phone.*

It pings.

Steven   Great work sunshine. Speak the truth.

@WeAreThePeopleAndItsArmy.

He presses his phone, a video from the **@WeAreThePeople AndItsArmy** *account plays.*

@WeAreThePeopleAndItsArmy *enters.*

@WeAreThePeopleAndItsArmy   Hello, my name is Micky Millen and I'm a truth-speaker for the British people and I will speak regardless of how it makes other people feel.

Ask yourself when did we stop recognising our own country and when did we stop supporting our own nation?

This isn't about hate, this isn't about race.

The reality is we have became second in our own country.

We are watching the systems that we built be handed to people who have never handed a thing to this country whilst those who work the hardest –

The builders, the nurses and the every day Brits, we get pushed to the back of the queue and the worst part is we're told to shut up and accept it.

But I won't. And we won't.

Because this is a warning shot that the people of this country are awake. We see what's happening. And we will not be ignored.

Not with hate. With heart. We love this country.

Enough to fight for it.

Check out my page and this week's video of the month,
a cracking example made beautifully by Steven Mooney
from Blyth.

Steven   @StevenFilmsBlyth followed back.

Scene 7

Neil Diamond's 'Forever in Blue Jeans' plays.

Ange *enters (in Blue Jeans, it's Thursday).*

Angela   The club night was a bit of a setback so I went back
to the drawing board. Back to absolute basics.

I couldn't get dinosaurs out of my head at the minute and
I realised it must be because all the really young lads were
always pretending to be them in the yard.

I grew up in the 80s and looking back to all the
young men then who was the hero that inspired
them most?

Well Indy, of course.

A leather jacket wearing, whip cracking, gun slinging
archeologist.

So put these two blindingly obvious inspirations to young
men together and what do you get?

That's right, a day out at the Hancock Museum. See the
dinosaur bones, look at some mummies, get inspired
by history.

That'll sort them out. Put life in perspective. I got onto Dirk
who also runs a bus company.

Dirk the DJ *enters.*

Dirk 'Travels ya thing and ya need a bus to Yirk, pick up the blower and buzz Dirk.' I couldn't think of a better rhyme so York was pretty close . . .

Beat.

Anyway . . . How many bairns yee wanting to get across, like?

Angela   I'd love to try and get about fifty lads brought.

Dirk   Whey, I've got the motor just for you, hinny. A lovely double decker. A right big red bastard.

Dirk *spits on the floor and exits.*

Angela   I got all the permissions from the school, got the head of history Mr Thomas to get involved too. We had a free coach and museum entry was free as well. It would be a mega inspiring day for them all.

The lights change, the Jurassic Park theme starts to play. **Angela** *puts on a fedora.*

Angela   I could see it now. Me leading the young lads through the dinosaur exhibition. This was me dad's hat, he always said that any good man should have a good fedora, just in case.

Two dinosaurs enter.

Angela *strokes them. Obviously.*

Angela   The boys would be so blown away by the day and the interesting facts about how big the dinosaurs were, and how they had feathers and stuff, their guards would be down.

I would be able to individually take them aside, arm round the shoulder sort of thing.

Chat to them about everything. Anything.

How home was, what were the day-to-day pressures they faced. Get them talking. Talking always helps. Show them some love. Know that they are here and they exist and that they have a bright future ahead.

The streets of somewhere like Blyth are hard and that they have things so many people couldn't imagine to deal with, but that set them up to fight life and to look after one another and be the very best men they could possibly be. And give them a good education at the same time.

One of the dinosaurs picks up a leaf blower (God knows where from) and blows it onto **Angela***, making her hair flap in the breeze as she stands with the dinosaurs triumphantly imagining being the hero she wants to be.*

Then. . .

The stage becomes chaos. The Jurrasic Park theme becomes techno-fied.

Angela   Unfortunately, things don't go to plan. Young Alan from Year 6 comes up in a huge rash from being dared to sit on top of a woolly mammoth. In the confusion, I don't spot Jonathan Howe and Ricky Spence break into one of the mummy cases. Bandages bloody everywhere. Steven Mooney thinks this is hilarious and films the whole bloody thing so all the faculty know about it instantly. Mr Thomas has a meeting with the the head to discuss me 'Staying in my lane' with the kids next school year.

A school bell rings.

The bell goes for the summer holidays. I put my fedora back in its hat box and book the next Friday night National Express that goes all the way to Victoria, London.

Dirk *enters.*

Dirk   Not want a lift, boony lass?

Angela   Nah, wanna be by myself for a bit.

Angela *and* **Dirk** *exit.*

Steven *appears. He's nowhere. The internet.*

Steven   So what made you want to do this? To become a more public figure?

@WeAreThePeopleAndItsArmy   Similar to you really.

Steven   What do you mean?

@WeAreThePeopleAndItsArmy   Well, I wanted the rest of the UK, the people at the top, to see for their own eyes just what we were living with. Our towns decimated. Forgotten. And why? Because we are being replaced. Politicians don't stand up for us. We need as many people for the cause as possible. To join our army.

Steven   I'm not really interested in politics.

@WeAreThePeopleAndItsArmy   That's what they want you to be like. To join the herd. A sheep.

Steven   I don't know mate. I'm only eighteen.

@WeAreThePeopleAndItsArmy   I got involved in all of this when I was fourteen. Lads on my estate had enough. Started organising rallies. I watched on. Older lads who couldn't get a job whilst vermin not from here were housed in hotels. Made me sick. (*Beat.*) Look, we need someone with your skillset.

Steven   I . . .

@WeAreThePeopleAndItsArmy   What's next? Because where you're from, where we're from. There's nothing next. Possibility of a job as a collections advisor in a call centre. But that's as dizzying as it'll ever get for someone like us. You're someone with clear talent. We can nurture that. We can help monetize that. That last video you didn't make a penny from, am I right?

Steven   No, nothing . . .

@WeAreThePeopleAndItsArmy   We can get you all set up to monetize. The following we have, we can give you a living. A purpose. A chance to be part of something. Feel like we're properly doing something.

Steven   Can I sleep on it?

@WeAreThePeopleAndItsArmy   Of course, sunshine. Of course. But I have to warn you. The clock's ticking. Things are going to get much, much worse.

Scene 8

Blyth town centre.

A news report.

'And there is Sir Keir Starmer who will become Britain's fifty-eighth Prime Minister.'

Caroline *enters.*

Caroline   I left Blyth when I was eighteen. I wanted something else. I remember when I was young, like really young the place being happy.

Bustling market stalls and my mam talking to the neighbours in the summer through thick bushes with little squishy white flowers attached.

A shop that sold everything by its weight, old school, washing powder, cereal, pick 'n' mix. Days in Ridley Park without a care in the world. Go and play.

Hot summer nights, woods like jungles full of adventure and Mr Eddy's ice cream van with the tune of Blaydon Races jingling through the streets. A friendly Italian face pushing snow-white Mr Whippy through a contraption that made it come out looking like spaghetti. And plenty of monkeys' blood.

Parents that were happy.

My dad smelling like Regal cigarettes, a brightest blue uniform for the factory he worked at on the coast road. Content. Fixed. Purpose. Place.

Power.

But something changed.

Beat

At fourteen.

The weighing house closed, Dad made redundant from the factory on the coast road and the jingle of Blaydon Races felt more jarring, more jagged.

That fizzing feeling too many times when you went to tap your card onto a bus knowing that you were on the precipice. Funds empty. That was what started the pull. The fight back. My fight back. My power. Marches. Petitions. A fight for my people.

When Mam moved out I knew I had to do the same.

I can't do this anymore. A bigger picture.

My mam lives up in Ponteland in a dead nice house with her second husband Martin.

When I come back I choose to stay here.

In my hometown because it still has its pull. But my fights are elsewhere now.

Beat.

Its power, deep inside.

That power that forged steel monsters and dived deep for black gold and reached the FA Cup fifth round.

That power is still here.

Still deep inside.

Its crackling, jagged.

Like electricity. But not the type a Durham male ballerina would sing about.

It's opaque.

Alive. Frightened.

And if it doesn't leave.

If it doesn't escape.

Then where does it go?

What does it do?

Scene 9

A London pub. **Angela** *sits.*

Neil Diamond's 'Red Red Wine' plays.

Angela I needed some space. A weekend away. A weird looking tent with a hot tub attached in the arse end of Durham? No thanks, for me I needed the hustle and bustle. To get lost in tourist traps, bright lights of Shaftesbury Avenue in the evening, wankers in suits clinking pints of Guinness, 'Split the G, split the G, split the G'. My hometown. London town.

A sprint around the boozers of central, then an overground home, Tottenham Hale. More boozers. That smell of spices filling the air as a cacophony of different people stuck together in God's country, like a Foster's-soaked matchbox with a sprinkle of cumin. Three of the lads I went to school with sat at the bar of the Volunteer Pub, a stone's throw from the station.

London Geezer   Ange, our girl! Where the fuck have you been all our lives?

Angela   The London sun slowly hiding behind the bottom window ledge, revealing the dust particles on the wood trim framing the butter yellow wallpaper. The white dust particles on the top of one of the lads' ragged facial hair glistening.

London Geezer   Me and the lads just been saying, we've got a spare for tomorrow. Pre-season game at Hearts, would be closer to your new gaff. What do you say? Trip to watch the mighty whites in Scotland? Coach picks us up here at 9am, match at 7pm, drop you off at Geordieland on the way back?

A bus arrives.

It's now the morning.

Angela   The usual 'banter' takes place on an away day football bus. Cans at 9am. Some suspicious packages being handed around. A tin can of lads all farting and burping beery burps. But there's loads of Greggs on offer. So my adoptive Geordie side is very happy. The topic of the new government and one of the lads' personal battle with social housing is quickly jettisoned as the chants start. Songs about the club's history, current players and their new manager from Australia. And then one I remembered from back in my youth.

An offensive Jewish word beginning with Y. The bus came to a halt. And the driver stood up, taking his cap off. Dirk?!

Dirk *enters.*

Dirk   Hey bonny lass, what are yee doing on here?

Angela   Went home for a couple of weeks and ended up here to go and see Spurs play. This one of yours?

Dirk   Aye, got a ton of work this pre-season between London and Scottish clubs. Anyway, which big bastard started that chant off? Come on, let's see ya?

Angela   A hand went up at the back and Dirk walked up the bus.

Dirk *sits amongst the lads.*

Angela   He went onto explain why the chant was used back in the day. The fact Tottenham was a large Jewish area and a huge proportion of the fans were from that background. Opposition fans would sing horrific chants to them, some of the most horrific stuff I'd ever heard.

Dirk   So instead of rejecting their Jewishness, they reclaimed the word and that's why they'd sing it proud. But today the fan base is a real mix of people, so it is not your word to reclaim.

Angela   The lads nodded in agreement. What had I just witnessed? Football teaching history teaching men to do better? Obviously it took a bloke to tell them mind so they'd bloody listen, but it was lush to watch. Dirk's a good egg nowadays.

Dirk   I've been around lass. Next stop, Edinburgh!

We snap to:

Caroline *and* **Steven** *enter.*

Steven   Just leave me alone. I don't need it.

Caroline   You've always been a fuck up, ever since we were little.

Steven   Caroline, man . . ./

Caroline   No, I'm not having a brother of mine be known for this sort of shit, I'm not having you bring me down with you.

Steven   Bring you down, you're doing that yourself, you've already went and got yourself a criminal record with your wanky posh friends gluing yaself to roads.

Caroline   Fuck you. I'm fucking fighting for something.

Steven   Just leave me alone.

Caroline   You'll never make it in film, you know that? Just like footy, you were destined to be the best, but you make shit decisions, you are always going to be a failure, left to rot here. Shelled out like this shit hole.

Steven *exits, kicking something as he leaves.*

Caroline *has a moment and then exists.*

Avicci 'Addicted to You' plays.

Angela   I hadn't been to a footy stadium since I was with me dad in White Hart Lane. It had hurt to be in one. But this time felt different. Just pure escapism. A reason to feel somewhere else. Tynecastle Stadium. Edinburgh. July 2024. The day I saw him. On the touchline, wrapped up snug in his grey suit, like a big Australian wombat. All warm yet grizzled. Eyes watery, beard bristly, stance strong. Tottenham Hotspur's new manager Ange Postecoglou. It all made sense. It all made sense.

I had come here to escape. The lads on the bus had learnt something through a match day. And there he was. My namesake. What I had to do. God, I knew what I had to do. What was my destiny? What my destiny is! Help the boys. Use footy to help them. A place to escape. Just pure escapism. I am him and he is me! I had to become a football manager! Manage the school team. To make the boys escape! I had to become Big Ange!

The song beat drops.

An array of grey-suited dancers with Ange Postecoglou masks enter.

They dance around **Angela**.

She joins in.

Complete bliss.

Angela *has a moment then exits.*

A flat in Blyth.

The music continues.

The atmosphere gets darker.

The dancing boys lose all of their joy.

They stand. Listening.

Caroline *is watching the news.*

TV Reporter   Tonight in this community that sense of shock is matched by disbelief that a summer holiday activity aimed at such young children could be targeted in this way.

Caroline *bursts into to tears.*

Upstairs in the flat.

Steven *is sitting on his bed.*

Messages pop.

Forums fizz.

The Boys *put on balaclavas.*

'*We said this was coming.*'

'*This is England.*'

'*We need to fight.*'

He reads them all.

They overcome him.

@WeAreThePeopleAndItsArmy *enters.*

@WeAreThePeopleAndItsArmy   Are you in?

Steven   My niece is one year old. I need to keep her safe. I'll do it.

@WeAreThePeopleAndItsArmy   This is a call to arms. This is war.

A fizz and a crackle of electricity fills the space.

@WeAreThePeopleAndItsArmy   Are you ready?

Steven *is pulled into the* **@WeAreThePeopleAndItsArmy** *by the dancing boys as the music comes to and end, he disappears with them and they exit.*

Left on the stage is **Angela**'s *fedora in a spotlight.*

End of Act 1.

Act Two

Scene 1

Angela *enters, she's got a brand new get-up, a full football manager's tracksuit and long Arsène Wenger-esque coat.*

She starts to put out some cones.

Several of **The Boys** *enter,* **Steven** *is one of them.*

The Boy Ange? Where's Micky Cairns? He normally coaches us for the summer tournament.

Angela He's missing this year. Went to Dubai with his family. Wife said it was footy or their marriage this year so he had no choice. She was offered too good a deal to go for the four of them. It was a once in a lifetime offer.

Dirk *enters.*

He's a travel agent.

Dirk So it's full board, you get entry to all the theme parks for the kids, all that baggage allowance and thirty drinks vouchers. It's once in a lifetime, cheaper than Tenerife.

Dirk *exits.*

Angela (*to the audience*) Dirk also owns a travel agents.

Dirk *re-enters.*

Dirk 'Ryanair and easyJet driving you beserk? Pick up the blower and buzz Dirk.' Get in! I'm back, baby!

Dirk *exits.*

The Boy But Ange, man, you don't know nowt about football.

Angela I've always followed it, never missed an England game, had a season ticket to Spurs when I was younger with me dad.

Until . . .

She stops.

Steven   I know, but Micky had coaching badges . . .

Angela   Look, most school teams have a PE teacher or head of year as their manager; you got lucky having Micky, it was just a passion project for him. Let him enjoy his fortnight in the UAE.

The Boy   But Ange, man . . .

Angela   Lads, I know you. I've seen you every weekday for the last five years. I've been there when the going got tough.

The Boy   And the tough got going. We know, Ange. Nobody can forget your Ronan Keating assembly piece.

Angela   I loved him for a reason, and let that reason be love.

Steven   Seriously, Ange, what can you actually do to help us win this tournament and beat Newsham?

Angela   Oh, I have some ideas. . . .

'When the Going Gets Tough' by Boyzone plays.

The scene plays out as a typical 'boys and sports film montage'. It's hyper-masculine to the point of camp.

Angela *runs a series of training exercises to the backdrop of the music.*

The boys *do a relay but the relay sticks are rolling pins.*

The boys *do various stretches whilst balancing dinner trays.*

Angela *controls a dinner trolley as a fake defender as* **The Boys** *dribble against it.*

The boys *do bicep curls with ladels full of mash.*

They put on tabards instead of bibs.

Dirk *enters, he's the assistant manager. He makes* **The boys** *chase light beams with his tech equipment.*

Angela *has them in Gordon Brown masks using the Chancellor of the Exchequer's red briefcase as a weight.*

Dirk *plays the trumpet solo in the song, it's only right because he runs a music teaching school too.*

It's chaos, beautiful chaos. **The boys** *are creasing. A real bundle of togetherness.*

All except **Steven** *who is off and looking nervous.*

The song ends.

The Boy   Ange, man, how is any of this meant to help?

Angela   Look at your faces, you're buzzing ya little tits off.

Steven   Ya can't say that, man.

Angela   Summer holidays. I can add swears to me team talks. Right everyone, go and collect the cones up and put the ladels in that big steel pan and then it's three fast laps around the pitch.

The Boys *sigh.*

The Boy   Come on man, Ange, three times?

Angela   I want you happier, well-drilled and three times fitter than those Newsham lads!

The Boys *pull themselves together and run off, leaving* **Steven** *who slowly goes to leave behind them.*

Angela   Everything okay, young Steven Mooney? You didn't seem yourself today. I'm glad you got your wee camera out and did a bit of filming.

Steven   I'm fine . . . I'm fine, Ange . . .

Steven *exits.*

Ange *watches him leave.*

Scene 2

Caroline *enters.*

She watches a video on her phone.

@WeAreThePeopleAndItsArmy   And that's another video from our very own Steven Mooney. He's observing the truth. He's observing that this is now an invasion. They're everywhere. In our work places, our hotels, even on our kids' football teams. In three days' time they will pay. The people and its army will rise and fight back.

Angela *enters carrying a ball bag over her shoulder.*

Caroline   Where's Micky Cairns? Why do they have you doing this?

Angela   UAE. Family hols. Great deal. (*Beat.*) Can I help you?

Caroline   I'm Steven's sister.

Angela   Young Caroline? Is that you? It must be nearly ten years since I last saw you.

Caroline   I hadn't forgotten about you, Ange.

Angela   You were a little terror, always trying to nick brunch bars at break time.

Caroline   And you were a right pain in my arse.

Angela   You never liked me, did you?

Caroline   Nar, you were too busy trying to entertain the lads. Always defending them.

Angela   They're just easily influenced, they get pushed into things a lot more.

Caroline   And what about us women? Why is it that we don't get pushed so easily?

Angela   Because we always fight back, because we have always had to fight back, to get anything.

Caroline   Yeah . . . well . . . yeah but that doesn't excuse the lads and making it easier for them.

Angela   My dad always said the silliest of things. He didn't need to say the cleverest of things because it was so much easier for him. We have to say the cleverest of things just to be on their level. Or we play dumb to survive, to make them feel like they are more clever than us. Less threatened. We've had years having to do this.

Caroline   Yeah and why should women always have to pick up the pieces and just be better to just be equal?

Angela   Because we are still fighting. We have that fight and we need to keep the fire burning.

Caroline   I . . . Um . . .

Angela   Why are you here?

Caroline   Steven. I'm worried. He's getting involved in things he doesn't understand. Just to make a bit of cash, to join something.

Beat.

He's being groomed to be a mouthpiece for radical online groups.

Angela   What is he doing?

Caroline   Making films. Footage of Muslim families around town, showing the place looking like a shithole and making it look like it's their fault.

Beat.

Filming some of the lads in the team.

Angela   I knew something wasn't right today. Have you spoken to him?

Caroline   Of course I have, he won't listen. I'm his posh big sister who fucked off down south.

Angela   You lectured him?

Caroline   I told him what is right and what is wrong.

Angela   Look around. How does he know what is right and what is wrong? He's a clever lad but a clever lad cracks and sparks when they're stuck not knowing how to get it all out.

Caroline   I just want him to see he's doing wrong. He has to know what he is doing is wrong.

Angela   Maybe he needs his big sister from back when.

Caroline   What?

Angela   Maybe he needs to know that you going away for a better life didn't really stop you being his big sister.

Caroline   How do I do that?

Angela   Music and nostalgia and memories. And love.

Caroline   You're fucking tapped, you.

Angela   Maybe. (*Beat.*) I'll see you round.

Angela *goes to leave.*

Angela   Caroline. Remember who you are. You're a Blyth lass. But you're also a woman trying to help a man. We're not so different. We're women fighting. Because that's all we know.

Angela *exits.*

Caroline *stands confused.*

Scene 3

Steven *enters with his tripod.*

He sets up the camera pointing it at the audience.

He presses his portable speaker 'Tennyson' plays.

Steven *and* **@WeAreThePeopleAndItsArmy** *take turns to read from a speech demonising immigration. It is up to the reader/*

director to input what speech from history they choose to have here. There are plenty to choose from.

Scene 4

A flat in Blyth. A baby cries.

Caroline *enters.*

Caroline   Shhh shhh, my darling, it's okay. Mam's here. Mam will always be here.

She finds the TV remote.

Why don't I put on Mam's favourite film when she was little, it's all about a magical girl who goes to school for the very first time and has to use her magic to defeat lots of wicked people. She's smart and likes books and reading. You're going to be like her. A clever girl. A magic girl.

Matilda the film plays.

Music, Rusted Root 'Send Me On My Way' plays.

A **Journalist** *enters.*

Caroline*'s attention turns to them.*

Journalist   The attack took place in the early hours of the morning. All the windows were smashed and red paint was sprayed across the sofas and foyer. A security guard was on hand to witness and is obviously shaken this morning.

Caroline   That's terrible. And I bet the poor cleaners had to clean it up. On minimum wage, I bet.

The **Journalist** *looks at* **Caroline***, they can hear her in her head.*

Journalist   Yeah. It's always the same isn't it?

Caroline   Always, why do the far right always think smashing up their own town will make people listen? Vermin.

Journalist   Far right?

Caroline   Yeah. I mean it's blatantly obvious, and I know they're probably just reacting to some hyperbole online and they're probably young and uneducated but that's what we have to label them as. It's the only way to make them see what they're doing is wrong.

The **Journalist** *turns away from* **Caroline** *and back to reporting.*

Journalist   'Liars' and 'Free Palestine' were also found to be graffiti-ed on the outside of the building in the red paint.

The **Journalist** *drops the mic and exits.*

Caroline *sits and thinks, Matilda continues to play on the TV.*

Scene 5

Angela *enters, a whistle round her neck.*

Angela   Right boys, keep it tight, quick one-twos; tabards, think about that structure at the back and skins, it's all about an organised press, Wakey into that space behind Dang when Steven presses. Very good.

It had been an intense week so far. I mixed the really silly with the really organised to keep the boys wanting more. I can't say I was a leading expert on being a football manager but my reading light stayed on until late watching masterclasses and matches with analysis afterwards. I knew the key to everything was to make the boys feel good and help them in the way I've been wanting to help them for many years.

Dirk *enters, arm around* **Steven**.

Dirk   Steven is what you'd describe as a goal poacher. A striker who sits on the last defender waiting to sniff out any chance that comes. Always been a good finisher and not great with link up play so it's always been his favourite position ever since he was like nine. Ange had been watching videos on the attacking press, to summarise, when a defending team get the ball, the attacking team squeeze up to try and force a mistake, it has to be properly organised or the defensive team can just play the ball out, 'escape the press' and advance with the ball into the attacking team's half.

Angela   The lads were working hard, they were understanding everything I had come up with.

Dirk *glances at* **Angela**.

Angela   What?

Dirk   Angela may have brought the oranges and cuddles but it was me who came up with the actual training plan.

Angela   Well. Dirk helped. He had a UEFA coach badge from his years working in Nuneaton.

Dirk   I played county level as a bairn, would have made it if it wasn't for me back. And the stint in prison.

Dirk *spits on the floor.*

Dirk   But she asked me to be her right-hand man, the Tindall to her Howe. I was more the Peter Taylor to her Brian Clough with my knowledge. That's a little reference for the older viewers.

Steven   My eyes stung, I'd been up late editing a video, my body feeling heavier than normal.

Angela   The ball went out of play and the keeper played a quick one to the defender.

Dirk   This was one of the moments when we wanted to utilise the press. Hunt down as one, Jagdish being the quickest and best tackler to run forward and chase, Dang filling his gap and then Steven going to the right to play for any ricochet to potentially get a shot in goal.

Angela   The first bit worked great, Jagdish was off like lightning, Dang second, closing down the space so the defender couldn't play the ball.

Dirk   The defender hesitated. Didn't have a pass. And Jagdish came bounding in.

Angela   The ball bounced and went right, exactly in the space where Steven would be.

Steven   Except I wasn't. I didn't react. My brain and legs heavy.

Dirk   So the keeper came running and collected the ball. The attack didn't happen.

Angela   But it did. But not what we expected.

Dirk   Dang first said it.

Steven   Steven man, concentrate.

Angela   Then Jagdish.

Steven   Come on, Mooney man, be alert, be on guard!

Steven   I am on guard, you fucking dick heads. I am alert. I'm fucking more alert than any of these soft cunts here. Fuck off and stop telling us how we have to do things in our country. Fuck off back to yours!

A swift noise.

The players, **Steven**, **Dirk** *and* **Angela** *exit.*

@WeAreThePeopleAndItsArmy *enters.*

A spotlight.

@WeAreThePeopleAndItsArmy   Tomorrow morning. Across the UK. We make history. We change history.

Scene 6

Steven *sits in the changing room alone.*

Angela *enters.*

Steven   Don't.

Angela   Alright.

Silence.

After some time **Angela** *pulls out a ball and starts throwing it against the wall.*

Steven   Do you mind?

Angela *stops.*

Angela   Talk to me.

Steven *laughs to himself.*

Angela   Why not?

Steven   You're a fucking dinner lady who now thinks she's José Mourinho. Why would speaking to you help?

Angela   Because maybe I'll listen.

Steven   And then you'll judge. They always judge.

Angela   Not everyone is out to get you.

Steven *scoffs.*

Moment of thought.

Angela *pulls out a Bose speaker. She puts on a track. It's Neil Diamond, 'Sweet Caroline'.*

Steven   Fuck's sake, man.

Angela   One of the very best.

Steven   Can you just leave me alone.

Angela (*singing*)   Where it began. I can't begin to knowing, but then I know its growing strong.

Steven   Fucking hell.

Steven *mutters something derogatory under his breath.*

Angela (*singing*)   Hands! Touching hands!

Angela attempts to get **Steven** *to hold her hands and dance.*

He pulls away.

She continues to sing the song. Keeping the energy up.

Angela *sings the chorus of Neil Diamond's 'Sweet Caroline'.*

The song continues into the next verse.

Steven's *feet are tapping.*

Angela *gestures to them.*

Angela   Knew you'd like this number.

Steven   Whey, it's impossible not to. It's like the unofficial anthem of the English working class.

Angela   Written by an American.

Steven   Aye, but they know how to be patriotic, divvent they. Proper patriots.

Angela   How do you feel when it's on?

Steven   Happy. Proper happy. Like this feeling of everyone being happy. I remember after Covid when England got to the Euros final. Belting this out with the lads in Dang's back garden.

Steven *has a moment.*

Steven   Class.

Angela   And it's got your sister's name in it.

Steven   Aye. The lads always make a point to serenade her when she's about and it's on.

Angela   It was my dad's favourite.

Steven   Is he dead?

Angela   He is. He was a different dad when I was younger. Singing and being nice.

Steven   What happened?

Angela *continues with another line of Neil Diamond's 'Sweet Caroline.'*

Steven   Ange, man. What happened to him?

Ange *continues to sing. Another chorus.*

Angela   Come on, sing it, lad!

Steven *reluctantly starts to join in.*

The song fades out. They both look at each other. And smile.

Scene 7

Journalist   It started just a few streets away from where the attack took place. A demonstration outside a mosque quickly turned violent and protestors attacked police officers, injuring over fifty, burned a police van and attacked the mosque. The next day over one hundred protestors were arrested in London as demonstrations happened throughout the country in Manchester, Aldershot and Hartlepool. Posts on platforms such as Telegram indicate that further protests will happen today in the North East of England.

A flat in Blyth.

Caroline *enters with the baby carrier.*

She paces. Puts the baby carrier by the sofa.

The slamming of a door.

Steven *enters with his tripod.*

Caroline   Where's your kit?

Steven   Not going.

Caroline   It's massive though. A chance to get one over Newsham. Your last chance to make a mark in the history of Wensleydale School.

Steven   I've got other plans.

Caroline   The lads will be relying on you.

Steven   Bigger things.

Caroline   But who's gonna score the goals?

Caroline *picks up the TV remote and pretends it's a commentator's microphone.*

It's a long ball forward, Mooney as usual is the first to beat the defender, he takes on another one, and another, then does a Maradona past the goalkeeper and smashes the ball into the net! Get innnnnnnnnnn!!!!!

Caroline *drops the remote, runs round the room, ending on her knees with her shirt over her head celebrating.*

Steven   What the fuck are you doing?

Caroline *stands up, brushing herself off.*

Caroline   I'm just being me. The real me.

Steven   I don't understand what you're playing at but I'm off.

Caroline   Stop.

Steven   I can't.

Caroline   Think of everything we talked about.

Steven   I'm doing it for her.

Caroline   Please.

Steven   You don't understand.

Caroline   They're all lying. To you. Like I said

Steven   You're still lecturing me. You're still doing it. Send me on my way!

Caroline   I . . . this is not how this is meant to end!

Caroline *is interrupted by the baby crying.*

Caroline   Oh darling, I'm sorry, Mammy will put on a film for you. What about the one in the snow with the silly . . . ferret.

Caroline *puts on Ice Age on the TV. 'Send Me On My Way' by Rusted Root plays.*

Steven   I'm doing it all for her . . .

Caroline   What? What sense is there in that? You total . . .

Steven *goes to leave.*

Caroline   No . . . sorry. I didn't mean that. Please explain it to me. How you're feeling.

Steven   If you'd just get off your high horse for one second you'd have known that. I'm doing it so she has a better life to grow up in.

Caroline *composes herself. She wants to explode but she doesn't.*

Caroline   Talk to me. I'm your big sister, Steven.

Steven   You're down there. You don't see what it's actually like here. At first I did think it was just a load of racists but then it started to make sense. My videos, in the comments, yeah, there were some scary people, but the majority, the majority were just normal people. Normal people like the people we see around Blyth. They are angry, they feel like they are being replaced, they have nothing, Caroline, they have fucking nothing, if I can help change that, if I can help give them something and give kids, kids like her, a chance. Then it's worth it. All of it. No matter what you or the high and mighty think. You think it's hate. It's not. It's wanting summat better for the bairn. You lot march for justice – I'm ready to bleed for it.

Caroline   Steven. I understand. This place. This place changed when we were growing up. It was different back then.

The town centre died, the people with not much now had nothing, it's what made me want to leave. Hell, it's why

Mam wanted a better life. But it's for other reasons than you think, it's bigger than all of this.

Steven   Kids are being killed now, Caroline, surely that's the endgame.

Caroline   There are evil people everywhere. Hell, there are evil people born in Blyth. We have to push up and not push down.

Steven   You mean like you acting all high and mighty because you've now joined the middle class elite down south?

Caroline   Exactly like that. We naturally push down. It's survival instinct. But we have to push up. We're frightened. We're cracking. But we have to push up.

A knock at the door.

Caroline *goes to answer it.*

Dirk *enters.*

Dirk   Ange sent me, after yesterday she thought you might have to be bundled into a bag to get you to the match in one piece.

Steven   I'm not going, Dirk.

Dirk   Thought you might say that.

Beat

I've been watching your videos. You've got a hell of a career ahead of you making films.

Steven   I've got to go, I'm going to be late.

Dirk   You know why Ange tells the stories about her dad and Neil Diamond? It's a front. It's so she only talks about the happier times with him. Before she had to cut him out of her life.

Steven   And why was that?

Dirk *thinks and doesn't answer the question directly.*

Dirk   See at the back end of the eighties we faced a similar battle. Nobody had work and an influx of people started popping up in our communities. We blamed them because that's what we saw. That was all we had in shot. I met Ange's dad in prison. He died before he got out. I got out and I turned my life around. It was hard. Had to become a bit of a wheeler-dealer. But that life made me meet lots of different people from all places and it made me understand that the problems were a lot bigger than I had first thought. Don't get me wrong, I didn't become a loony lefty . . . sorry.

Caroline   I'll let it stand.

Dirk   Thanks. But I changed dramatically. Surrounded myself with beautiful people. Mainly decent women, like Ange, who just wanted to help and make me see the world in a different way. Never judged me. Realised my background made it very difficult to see anything else. When you tell a young bloke from a council estate in Blyth that he is privileged and that other people deserve more than him then he's going to get angry. Because he's worked hard to get just a scrap. He's told he has to work hard. Because he's the man of the house. The provider. And he's also a fighter. But he has to fight in different ways.

Steven   That's what I'm doing though, I'm fighting in a different way. And I'm late to this particular fight.

Steven *goes to leave.*

Dirk   You are, Steven. What are you really fighting for? What does your sister fight for? It's the same thing you know. It's just you're looking through a different lens.

Steven *exits. As he leaves he picks up a bag.*

Dirk *looks at* **Caroline**.

Caroline   What happens now?

Dirk   You let him choose his path. You've done everything you could.

Caroline   It's always up to us lasses, isn't it?

Dirk   It is. But don't tell him that.

Scene 8

Angela *enters.*

'Glory Road' by Neil Diamond plays.

Angela *takes her dad's fedora out of a box and looks at it.*

A noise.

The music distorts into Avicci 'Addicted to You'.

Ange Postecoglou *enters.*

Angela   Did Dirk tell them about my dad?

Big Ange   Sort of, mate.

Angela   And is Steven coming to play the final?

Big Ange   Not sure, mate.

Angela   I am doing it for him, you know.

Big Ange   I know, mate.

Angela   See, if he hadn't fallen in with that wrong crowd, if he had just been shown some love, then that hatred wouldn't have burned in him. It's why I try and give the boys love, every single day.

Big Ange   Angela. You, like most Sheilas, didn't have stacks of role models and you did alright, didn't you, mate?

Angela   My dad was my role model. Before . . .

Big Ange Just say it, mate.

Angela Before he joined the English Defence League. Before he went to prison. Before he . . .

Big Ange See, mate.

Angela See what?

Big Ange You couldn't have done anything, you doing what you do now is already more than enough. It's not up to Sheilas to always fix things, you know, mate?

Angela Can you stop saying Sheilas?

Big Ange Sorry. I'm a really really accentuated stereotype, mate.

Angela Will it always be this difficult?

Big Ange Keep listening to Neil, still visit the footy, just because something turned sour it doesn't mean you can't still like the good in it, mate.

Angela Maybe . . . mate.

Big Ange There's a good Sheila.

Angela *gives a telling off look to* **Ange Postecoglou**.

Angela I knew there was good in him, you know. Dirk told me the stories when they shared in that cell. He wanted to change what he had done. He was taught to blame the problems on people who had nothing. Dirk was the same and look at him now. I just wanted my boys to feel something.

Big Ange Empathy, mate?

Angela Yes. (*Beat.*) What happens next?

Big Ange Play the final. With or without Steven. I had to do my first whole year without Harry Kane, mate.

Angela Now that is true.

Big Ange   And maybe this isn't the time for it to happen. I always used to say I always win in my second season, mate.

Angela *picks up her dad's hat again.*

The Boys *enter in their football strips, all but* **Steven***.*

Angela *takes another look at the hat. To* **Ange Postecoglou***. They smile.*

Steven *enters in another place. On a Metro.*

The sounds of it moving play out. The tannoy of 'Next stop the Stadium of Light'.

Steven   A young mam across from me picks up her baby. She smells its bum and pulls a face. I laugh. We meet eyes. She laughs too. I think about Dirk and Ange and her dad. I think about my dad. About when we were younger and how he had a job. How he was in the house with us as kids. Me and Caroline. Caroline. I think of my niece. Why I'm doing this. I'm doing this for her. I'm doing this for her?

The beep of Metro doors opening.

Steven *goes to leave but drops his bag. A camera lens falls out.*

He picks it up. Looks at it and exits.

Back to **Angela***.* **Postecoglou** *is gone and it's just* **Angela** *and her boys.*

Angela   Right, let's do this!

'The Nights' by Avicci plays.

The stage becomes a football pitch.

The Boys *get in to a huddle. In the middle* **Angela** *leads the team talk, she has her fedora back on.*

The Boys   We are Blyth! We are Blyth! We are Blyth!

Steven *enters, he is another place. Sunderland.*

The Boys *become rioters.*

The Boys   We want our country back! We want our
country back! We want our country back!

Steven *is amongst them, he is unsure. He tries to shake it off.*

Caroline *enters with her baby.*

Steven *looks at them both. A moment.*

Caroline *exits.*

Steven *goes to set up his camera, in a brawl* **The Boys** *knock it
out of his hands. The lens again takes his gaze.*

@WeAreThePeopleAndItsArmy *enters.*

He stands face to face with **Steven**.

The music drops.

@WeAreThePeopleAndItsArmy *exits.*

Chaos breaks out.

In amongst it **Steven** *is battered and bruised.*

Dirk *enters. In the past. Waving a St George's flag. Big anger.*

Steven *looks back at* **Dirk**.

Caroline *enters. She is here, in the moment.*

Caroline   Steven Alexander Mooney.

Steven   No. You shouldn't be here.

Caroline   Matilda or Ice Age?

Steven   I . . .

Caroline   Matilda . . . or Ice Age?

The world goes back four years.

We see a passing of time.

*The hooligans turn into young boys in shirts and ties, sipping J2Os
with little trophies in their hands.*

Caroline *looks younger.*

A presentation night for the football. She's nineteen and **Steven** *is fourteen.*

Steven *carrys a trophy.*

A disco plays out. Rusted Root 'Send Me On My Way' plays.

Caroline   There he is, players' player of the year – STEVEN ALEXANDER MOONEY!

Steven   Give over.

Caroline   Come on, have a dance with your big sister.

Caroline *dances a bit with* **Steven**.

Steven   Get off is, you're embarrassing is, man.

Caroline   Ah, is that because Jagdish's sister has been staring at you all night?

Steven   I don't know what you're talking about.

Caroline *puts some food in her mouth.*

Caroline   Steven . . .

Steven   What?

Caroline   Bleurghhh.

Caroline *chases* **Steven** *around with mushed up food in her mouth, eventually, she swallows it.*

Steven   You're a bloody weirdo, you know that.

Caroline   I have to be the one who humbles you, that's my job. Teach you the way of the world, occasionally fart under your duvet and always have your back.

Steven   Nobody else's sister acts like you.

Caroline   That's because they don't have the most talented younger brother who is going to do amazing things in life.

I might even have to start hurting you to make sure people can't hurt you worse later in life!

Steven   Dad was worried today, where were you?

Caroline   You're too young to understand these things, man.

Steven   I want to know. Dad's a sad man, Caroline.

Caroline   I was outside the factory. I joined a few of the other guys who'd lost their jobs. I stood there for Dad. Never done anything like it before.

Steven   What were you doing, though?

Caroline   I was taking a stand. To the bastards at the top. They made Dad sad. They took it all away from him.

Steven   I don't understand?

Caroline   There'll be plenty of time for that. Guess what? I got you tickets for Bond, No Time To Die. Me and you, Odeon, Silverlink, the proper posh seats that recline.

Steven   Honestly?

Caroline   Yep.

She starts to mimic M in James Bond.

That which we are we are, one equal temper of heroic hearts made weak by time and fate!

Steven   Who was that meant to be?

Caroline   Judi Dench. M. From Skyfall.

Steven   Shite impression.

Caroline   Wew . . . Do you recognise this song?

Steven   Yeah, it's from Ice Age.

Caroline   What?! No it's not, it's from Matilda.

Steven   It's definitely Ice Age.

Caroline   Eh, nah, I can see her now with her mousey bob making the breakfast cereal dance around the kitchen.

Steven   I can see it now, when the ferret, the lion and the elephant take the baby on the long journey ahead.

Caroline   He's a sloth, Sid the sloth.

Steven   Whatever, it's still that song.

Dirk the DJ *enters*.

Caroline   The DJ will know, excuse me, can you tell me what film this is from?

Dirk   Areet young uns, whey aye, I remember it from Pie in the Sky with John Goodman, cracking film, never got the plaudits it should have. A real clash of cultures about a traffic warden and an avant garde dancer. Real good stuff. Not like modern weird theatrical stuff that tries too hard to be funny and political at the same time.

Caroline   Thanks?

Dirk   Aye, and obviously you'll both know it from Ice Age and Matilda. Took me eldest to see Matilda at the pictures and me youngest to see Ice Age. That Sid the sloth, what a plonker.

Dirk *exits*.

Steven   Apology?

Caroline   Whey, we were both right.

Steven   I never said it wasn't from Matilda, I just said I knew it was from Ice Age.

Caroline   Soz. Truce?

Steven   Truce.

They embrace.

Caroline   Matilda or Ice Age?

We're back in the present, in the midst of the riot.

*She pulls **Steven** from the crowd.*

The Boys *become footballers again.*

Ange, **Steven** *and* **Caroline** *look out to the audience.*

The music ends.

The world centres.

A decision has been made.

Steven *now wears his football kit. Blackout.*

Scene 9

Dirk *enters, he sweeps up the mess,* **The Boys** *come running in carrying a trophy.*

The Boys   We've got our town back, we've got our town back, we've got our town back.

They exit apart from one boy, the boy from **Angela**'s *first speech.*

Dirk   Glory. Not much glory here. Fleeting.

The Boy *sighs.* **Dirk**'s *done this before.*

Dirk   Don't ever forget where you come from. Work hard, lad. Don't let the bastards get you down. Life's number one lesson. The people above are the real bad guys, remember that. Keep crackling.

The Boy *doesn't know what to say. Instead he points off, indicating he has to be somewhere and exits.*

Dirk *goes over to a record player in the corner of the room.*

Dirk   One last time this year, Neil.

'America' by Neil Diamond plays.

It's dramatic to begin with.

We see a flicker of **@WeAreThePeopleAndItsArmy**.

He disappears.

Then **Caroline** *and* **Steven** *embracing, a medal around* **Steven***'s neck.*

Then **Angela***. Through a tunnel of smoke. Lights, lasers if possible. The works.*

Dirk *controls it all from a booth at the side.*

Angela *is wearing a full Indiana Jones outfit, fedora leather jacket, whip, the lot. (And her winner's medal around her neck.)*

Angela   Truth is, none of us has the answer. We just keep chucking our colours in the air – red flag, white mask, glitter confetti – hoping summat sticks. You march, he rages, I put on sequins. Same fight, different daft weapons. All of us trying to beat back the same bloody hopelessness.

Dirk *joins her by her side. He's wearing a cap, à la Short Round from Indiana Jones.*

Angela   But we'd done something. That was true. A story rewritten. It's complex, you know. A mess. All of it.

She looks at **Dirk***. He squeezes her hand.*

Angela   But my summer was officially now about to start. But there was no way we were stopping there. Dirk signed us up to a proper coaching summer school in a college in America, they treat lasses' football dead seriously there. It's basically just like the ending of Bend It Like Beckham.

Dirk   We're off to America. And just like Indiana Jones, to work in a college and maybe fight some Nazis.

Angela   Not everyone who you disagree with is a Nazi, man Dirk. You should know better.

Dirk   Aye. But a few of bloody are. Dear America, move over Indiana! Dear England, move over Southgate!

Angela   Dear Dad . . . I . . .

She has no more to say.

Angela *and* **Dirk** *exit hand in hand.*

An image of Elon Musk appears.

The image of Musk flickers. Into a host of people from the UK, Laurence Fox, Calvin Robinson, then Tommy Robinson and finally into **@WeAreThePeopleAndItsArmy**.

He stares at the audience. Tilts his head.

An image of a bonfire with a small boat on the top of appears on the screen.

@WeAreThePeopleAndItsArmy *laughs uncontrollably.*

Caroline *enters.*

Caroline   It's complex, isn't it? Right now. We fight. We shout. We scream. A cacophony of noise. I see wars in places I will never set foot and my heart breaks for those people. Free Palestine.

I see people in my hometown who turn to food banks and are told that the reason they can't put on their heating is because of people below them. Free Blyth. I stand somewhere in the middle. Privileged. Yes. A woman in the West. Comme ci, comme ça.

She switches off the images making them all disappear and changes the record in the player.

@WeAreThePeopleAndItsArmy *can be heard laughing in the distance.*

Steven *enters.*

Steven   It's complex, isn't it. Right now. We fight. We shout. We scream. Free the hostages. Stop the boats. What is right? What is the right thing to say? What is left? What will be left? I stand somewhere in the middle. A lad from Blyth.

Privileged. Yes. But only sometimes. Talented. Obvs. Confused. Always.

He presses play on a device.

'Send Me On My Way' by Rusted Root begins to play.

They breathe out.

They smile at each other.

Blackout.